NASCAR
Champions

DALE EARNHARDT

Victoria Braidich

New York

Published in 2007 by The Rosen Publishing Group, Inc.
29 East 21st Street, New York, NY 10010

Book Design: Michael J. Flynn

Photo Credits: Cover (Earnhardt), pp. 11, 13 © Jamie Squire/Allsport; cover (background) © Robert Laberge/Getty Images; p. 5 © Craig Jones/Allsport; p. 7 © R. Gates/Getty Images; pp. 9, 17, 21 © David Taylor/Allsport; p. 15 © Bill Hall/Allsport; p. 19 © Erik S. Lesser/Newsmakers.

Library of Congress Cataloging-in-Publication Data

Braidich, Victoria.
  Dale Earnhardt / Victoria Braidich.
      p. cm. — (NASCAR champions)
  Includes bibliographical references and index.
  ISBN-13: 978-1-4042-3512-4
  ISBN-10: 1-4042-3512-4 (library binding)
 1. Earnhardt, Dale, 1951- 2. Stock car drivers—United States—Biography—Juvenile literature. I.
Title. II. Series.
GV1032.E18B73 2007
796.72092—dc22
(B)
                                        2006014305

Manufactured in the United States of America

Contents

Dale Earnhardt was a great race car driver. Some people say he was the best ever.

5

Dale's father Ralph was a race car driver. He raced cars in the 1950s and 1960s.

6

Dale's son Kerry is a race car driver. Dale's daughter Kelley raced for a while too.

Dale's son Dale Jr. is a race car driver too. Some people think he could be as good as his dad someday.

11

Dale started racing for NASCAR full-time in 1979. He was voted Rookie of the Year that year.

13

Dale won seven NASCAR championships! Only one other driver has ever done that.

14

Dale won the Daytona 500 in 1998. He had been in the race twenty times before winning it!

Dale died during the 2001 Daytona 500. Many NASCAR drivers and fans miss him.

I Love You!
Goodwrench
ale's final lap
In our hearts forever
Thanks for the memory
Racing
Gone but not forgotten
my HERO
hero

Dale is on NASCAR's list of the 50 Greatest Drivers.

20

21

Glossary

championship (CHAM-pea-uhn-ship)
A contest held to see who is the best
in a sport.

Daytona 500 (day-TOH-nuh FYV
HUN-druhd) The famous first NASCAR
race every year. It is held in Daytona
Beach, Florida.

rookie (RU-kee) Someone who is in their
first year in a sport.

22

Books and Web Sites

Books

Buckley, James. *NASCAR*. New York: DK Children, 2005.

Schaefer, A. R. *Dale Earnhardt*. Mankato, MN: Capstone Press, 2006.

Web Sites

Due to the changing nature of Internet links, PowerKids Press has developed an online list of Web sites related to the subject of this book. This site is updated regularly. Please use this link to access the list:
http://www.powerkidslinks.com/NASCAR/earnhardt/

Index